EFFECTIVE TELECOMMUTING

Learn how to work from home efficiently and productively

Written by Maïlys Charlier

Translated by Emma Lunt

Coaching 50MINUTES.com

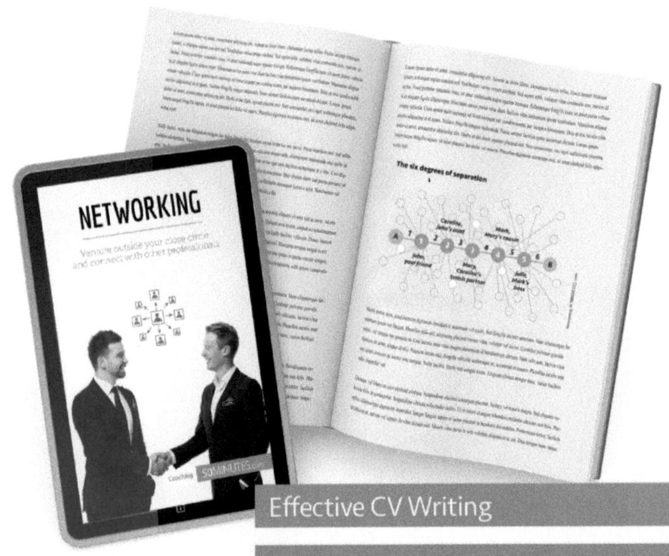

50MINUTES.com

PROPEL
YOUR BUSINESS FORWARD!

NETWORKING
Venture outside your close circle
and connect with other professionals

Coaching   50MINUTES.com

The six degrees of separation

Effective CV Writing

Resolving Office Conflict

Boost Your Concentration

Find Your Work-Life Balance

www.50minutes.com

EFFECTIVE TELECOMMUTING

- **Issue:** how can I work effectively from home? What are the keys to time management when working from home?
- **Uses:** telecommuting presents a real challenge in terms of time management. Being self-disciplined at home will enable you to be as efficient there as at the office.
- **Professional context:** working from home, telecommuting, time management, personal organisation.
- **FAQs:**
  - What are the jobs which may require telecommuting?
  - Do I have to establish a specific contract?
  - Is telecommuting more relaxing than working at the office?
  - What should I do in the case of a computer or hardware malfunction?
  - What happens if there is a work accident?
  - What do I do when I am ill?
  - What are the aspects to consider before starting to telecommute (legal, practical, logistical and personal aspects, etc.)?

A relatively recent idea, telecommuting (working from home) is increasingly common. Thanks to the age of Web 2.0, smartphones and the many communication apps, it has become easy – for some jobs anyway – to work from home. Working from home is often considered an advantage: we gain time as we are spared the commute to work; we also avoid the fatigue of public transport or car journeys and their share of daily traffic jams; we save money by not buying fuel or transport tickets; we can organise our day as we wish; we are free to do what we want during our lunch break; we avoid the frequent interruptions and distractions of the office.

But telecommuting is not a synonym for lazing around. You must learn to manage your time and improve your organisation, as well as to reserve a space specifically dedicated to your career. Your employer will often be even more demanding when you work at home. By allowing you to work from home, they are trusting you and thus reasonably expect productive work in return. It is therefore a good idea to seriously consider all the ins and outs of such a decision.

> "I have always had difficulty concentrating. When my employer allows it, I prefer working from home so as to avoid as many distractions as possible. But telecommuting requires great self-discipline! It is really not easy to be productive and to provide the expected work while alone in the house." (Emily, publisher)

EFFECTIVE TELECOMMUTING: THE BASICS

THE VAGUE TERM OF TELECOMMUTING

According to UK law, telecommuting refers to any type of work that is done by an employee outside the organisation's premises on a recurring basis, with the help of computer technologies. Working outside the company's premises does not necessarily mean working from your home: there are types of telecommuting that take place in either a co-working space, or on trips for some jobs.

There are different types of telecommuting: nomadic work, which involves being constantly on the go and carrying out your work outside the organisation's premises (such as a salesperson or consultant); telecommuting at home, which involves working all week from home; part-time telecommuting, which is an alternative form of work meaning that the employee spends part of their time working from home and comes to work for some days within the organisation; and finally, collaborative work, which involves working on shared files with people that are geographically far away and they do this with groupware (software programmes that enable many people to share documents from a distance, such as Dropbox, Gmail, Skype, etc.).

This book looks at working from home and part-time telecommuting.

WHY WORK FROM HOME?

The good reasons

For the worker, this method of organising work, which may be practiced on a full-time basis or one or two days per week – the rest of the time being spent at the organisation – presents numerous advantages.

- The worker will, theoretically, benefit from an all-around increase in quality of life (more time for themselves, satisfaction, motivation, better physical shape, etc.).
- The time saved by not commuting can be used for other things, like having an extra hour's sleep, doing some sport in the morning, meditating, etc. This has a significant impact on health.
- They will suffer from less interruptions and distractions that can happen in a classic working environment (colleagues, open plan, etc.).
- As the employee is in a calmer environment, they will be more able to concentrate and, in theory, will be more productive.

> "I've noticed that when I work from home, I am much more efficient and quick. It is easier to concentrate at your own house than at the office where it is difficult to think properly if a colleague is on the phone right next to you or when your colleagues are chatting together. At home, I am relaxed and nobody disturbs me." (Stephanie, journalist)

- They can save money on transport, meals, etc.
- Their motivation tends to increase as the employee is at

home and has more independence regarding time management and the organisation of their work.
- They will have greater flexibility in case of a personal
emergency, meeting, etc.
- Finally, telecommuting – if well organised – reduces
stress during the day (no never-ending commutes, no
stressed or stressful colleagues, etc.).

Advantages for a telecommuter

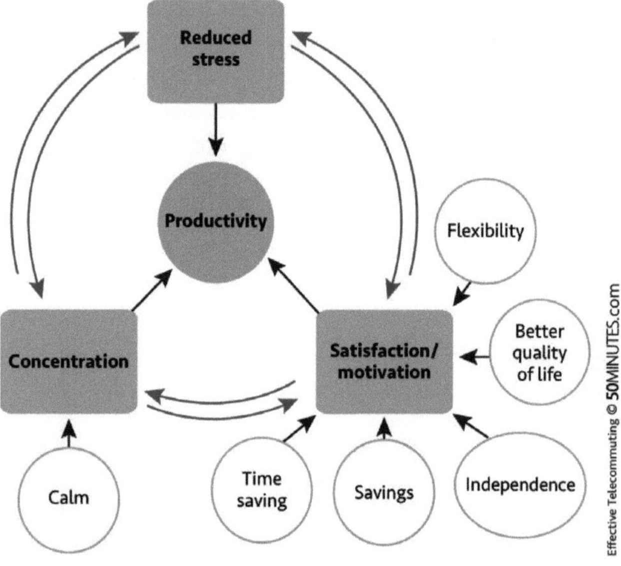

The employer also benefits from allowing employees who
wish to telecommute to do so.

- There is a distinct drop in absenteeism and presenteeism.

- Telecommuting also generates more time for real work on the part of the employee: they waste less time on transport and are therefore more willing to have less or shorter breaks.
- As the employee is at home, they generally demonstrate greater flexibility: they are easily inclined to change their schedule or to work outside office hours.

Significant disadvantages

As with any type of work, however, there are also disadvantages to working from home, as much for the employer as for the employee. Thus, for the employee, there are aspects that are more difficult to manage:

- implementing specific framework;
- difficulty of supervising;
- reduction in team cohesion;
- increased risks of endangering confidentiality;
- potential extra material costs.

DEFINING MEASURABLE INDICATORS

While it is difficult to control a telecommuter's working hours, their productivity level and their efficiency are more easily measurable. In fact, as the employee works from home, they can regularly send reports detailing the tasks done each day. Their employer will then be able to evaluate their performance directly.

Implementing a telecommuting system can also require a small investment from the telecommuter at the start, such as creating an at-home office. But the main disadvantages regard contact with colleagues, as well as personal organisation, which must be vigorous. We will come back to these points later.

BEFORE DIVING IN

A suitable working space

Working from home is not suitable for everybody. While telecommuting is clearly based on the mutual consent of the telecommuter and the employer, it is also necessary to consider the material aspect, as working from home requires a good computer system and an available office too. Is that the case at my house? Can I rely on these different aspects? Or on a nearby coworking space? Am I prepared to make the necessary adjustments? These questions are important, as it is unrealistic to think that you can manage your regular working days on the kitchen table; you need a dedicated space, which is well-lit and calm.

In terms of running costs, it would be wise to have a subscription with unlimited internet, at the risk of seeing your telecommuting costing you a small fortune! Furthermore, a limited connection will slow you down when doing tasks. Add telephone costs to this: you will certainly have to stay in contact with your colleagues and superiors. Nonetheless, all of this can be discussed with your employer, so as to agree to a reasonable reimbursement.

Personal reflection

It is also appropriate, and this is the essential point, to seriously consider the immense self-discipline needed for this type of work. Some people will be much more productive when they are alone at home, while others will be less efficient as soon as they leave the structure of an office. Working from home involves finding a different structure and pace of work. If you work at home in the same way as you do at the office, this solution will not be effective and you will not be able to be rigorous.

You therefore have to reflect on and ask yourself these questions beforehand: do I have good reasons for wanting to telecommute? Am I capable of getting by with computer software or other technological aspects if there is a problem? Does my job require additional training to be able to do it remotely? Am I prepared to be all the more available for my colleagues and my superior given that I work remotely? Am I capable of managing my timekeeping? Will I not be tempted or distracted by my private environment? Am I capable of managing my private life and my professional life under the same roof?

A professional contract

There are different legal aspects linked to telecommuting and they vary depending on the country you live in. One thing is certain: if the employee does not want to work from home, the employer cannot force them. This is reciprocal: if an organisation refuses to allow it, the employee cannot demand the right to telecommute from their employer. Furthermore, if telecommuting is not mentioned in the contract, the employer has to sign an additional clause with their employee so as to make the telecommuting legal. The two parties are thus protected in case of disputes or incidents. The additional clause will detail the equipment to be made available to the worker when they work from home.

EXTRA INFORMATION

Consider your insurance. It is worthwhile checking with your organisation if the equipment that you are given is insured against robbery, breakage or malfunction. Similarly, ask yourself what would happen if the equipment breaks down, or in the case of illness or a work-related accident, and check with your employer that there is a clause regarding this.

BEING WELL-ORGANISED WHEN TELECOMMUTING

The greatest challenge for a telecommuter will therefore be demonstrating self-discipline and a good separation between the time devoted to their job and that devoted to their private life, as the two occur in the same place.

EMPLOYER ADVICE

Telecommuting is also a challenge for the employer, who must also learn to trust their employee when they work from home. They must of course make the employee aware of their responsibilities, supervise them remotely and clarify the steps to follow during their days of telecommuting, but this process can only be carried out calmly and have a positive effect on the organisation if the employer puts their trust in their co-workers.

Good routines

The first routine to establish when you are telecommuting is a daily routine, as if you were going to the office: get up when your alarm goes off, take a shower, get dressed, have breakfast. Act as if you are going to leave the house. This morning routine is essential to begin an effective, 'normal' working day. If you stay in your pyjamas or slippers, you will subconsciously want to laze around or go back to bed; you will struggle to find the motivation to get to work.

Working space

It is important to have a closed space with a desk so as to isolate yourself from daily life in the house and its temptations. This working space must have sufficient light, be calm and be as far as possible from distractions like outside noise, smells from the kitchen, etc. It is also useless to plan to work in bed or on the sofa because you will not do anything productive. Working at your desk also enables you to have all your documents and tools for working within arm's reach. If you make a daily habit of telecommuting, you should ensure the ergonomics of your working area (an adapted desk chair, for example) so as to avoid health problems. Finally, if you do tasks for work on computing equipment from the organisation, it is better to do your personal activities on your own equipment.

A concrete schedule

Given that there is no hierarchy at your house, you are the boss. But just because you work from home does not mean that you can give yourself a lie-in or different working hours. Yet the temptation will be immense. Ensure, particularly at first, to set fixed hours and to respect them so that you get used to your new 'freedom' and do not let your work invade your private life and vice versa. Not only is it more professional to stick to office hours, but working at the same pace as your colleagues will bring you closer to them and enable you to be more productive. It would be counterproductive, for example, to neglect a lunch break. Coordinate yourself with your co-workers so that you eat at the same time as them.

Nevertheless, this does not mean that you have to keep exactly the same hours as before, as you will save time by no longer commuting. Use this new time however you see fit (an extra hour in bed, sport, painting, reading, etc.), but make your days ritual so that you are not distracted.

It is up to you to establish a reasonable schedule as well as a to-do list, and to stick to it. While you are advised to keep to a traditional schedule, on the other hand it is better not to plan your tasks in the same way as when you are at the office. Indeed, when you work from home, your pace is not the same: for example, you need less time in the morning before starting your day. You will therefore theoretically be less alert than if you had made the journey to work. Consequently, consider starting your day off gently and varying tasks according to this new pace.

Take particular care to prioritise and define daily goals that are feasible to do in one day of work so that, on the one hand, you stay motivated by seeing the work you have achieved – like a traditional day at the office – but even more so that your superiors can see a real advance in the work that you are doing beyond the office walls. Also note down everything you have done during your telecommuting hours.

You should also plan regular breaks. It is not actually rare for a telecommuter to feel guilty for leaving their work station, when they did not think twice before doing it at the office. It is, however, important – necessary even – to take breaks at home as well. As you would do at your place of work with your colleagues, take time for a coffee or tea. Remember to warn the office when you take a break, either by simply putting yourself as 'absent' on the instant messaging service or by writing to them directly.

The advantages of telecommuting

We were just talking about traditional breaks, but you can do far better: make the most of the advantages you have by staying at home! Use your lunch break to do a household chore, play sport, indulge in your passion or go to do the grocery shopping. Getting some fresh air and being busy with something else will allow you to return to work with better concentration and motivation. Do not stay sat in front of your computer all day. Conversely, take advantage of the chance you have to get up frequently without disturbing people: stand up to make a phone call, drink tea, to go and throw some paper in the bin.

You have another advantage: the possibility of changing your working environment if you so wish. So, do not hesitate to leave your house to set up in a café, at the house of a friend who also works from home, at a library close to your home, etc. You will obviously have to adapt your tasks accordingly, based on the equipment or concentration necessary.

Concentration equals productivity

It is not always easy to remain focused. When you are at home, while it is true that you no longer have to put up with interruptions from colleagues and the distractions that come from the hubbub of an office, other factors are likely to distract your attention from your work tasks. In order to get by, the key is to keep planning your activities well.

Therefore, if you have children or if your partner returns from work before you have finished your day, considering planning to do tasks that require more concentration when you are alone or, if this sort of schedule suits you, once your children have gone to bed. Furthermore, consider generally alternating complicated tasks with mindless tasks, which will help you to really make the most of your brain's ability throughout the day.

Furthermore, you are strongly advised not to believe that you can do all your tasks for work correctly while looking after the house, the puppy, the baby or the children if they have returned or are ill. You cannot be everywhere at the same time. Wanting to control everything at once is like running straight at failure or burnout, because it is definite that something will be done at the expense of something else. This is why clear distinction is still the best option for remaining focused. If you absolutely have to attend to your private life for one reason or another, do not count this as working time and postpone your working tasks until a more suitable time, or take a day off depending on your employer.

Your loved ones' involvement

It is essential to establish a 'contract' with your loved ones. Your family, your partner, your children, if they are around, have to understand that when you are sitting at your desk, it is as if you were at work. Impose rules so that they do not come and disturb you during your working hours. You are not available and those around you cannot interrupt you at any time. This also goes for your friends and family that are free during the day: they must not think that because you are at home, they can contact you whenever or pop by for a cup of tea. In the same way that they would not call you numerous times per day when you are at the office, they cannot come and disturb you during your telecommuting hours.

Following the same idea, be sure to make everybody who lives under the same roof as you understand that just because you are at home does not mean you suddenly have lots more free time to do chores; feel free to do a quick urgent trip to the grocery store during your break, but not a big spring clean on a day of telecommuting!

On the contrary, try not to let your working time overflow into your private life. Those around you will feel more at ease with the fact that you work from home if you do not neglect them in favour of extra hours or of working outside your regular time at work. When the day is over, switch off your computer and leave the room, as you would leave the office. If your hours change or are moved around, post them in the kitchen or outside so that your whole family knows when you are available and when you are not.

Make regular self-assessments

When you are a telecommuter, the difficulty comes from assessing yourself objectively. Given that a telecommuter answers to themselves, they are going to have to self-assess and do regular appraisals, and to rethink their organisation if they notice that they are not very productive.

In this way, from the first day of telecommuting, it is necessary to do an assessment, so as to check that you are going in the right direction and to immediately change course if necessary. Skim through your to-do list and evaluate what was done. Write down all your remarks and compare this inventory to the next so as to draw conclusions on your experience, to improve and to rectify what is not working. Following this, review regularly, ideally on a weekly basis, and do not hesitate to backtrack if something does not work or if your situation changes.

	Yes	No
Have you done all the tasks you had planned?		
Have you had good communication with your colleagues?		
Have you sent a report to your superior?		
Have you done any additional tasks?		
Have you observed your breaks?		
Have you crammed too much into your schedule?		

It is up to you to also see with your superior when is the best time to do an assessment together. Reviewing with your employer enables you to know whether your organisation or work is optimum and corresponds with what the organisation expects. But your employer will also be able to see the work you are doing when you are working from home.

THE RISKS FOR THE TELECOMMUTER

Beware of isolation

When we are often telecommuting, it is important to be aware of professional isolation, especially if we permanently work remotely. Thus, do not skip regular returns to the organisation to attend meetings or events organised among your colleagues. This will enable you to maintain good relations with them and to stay a part of the team.

And when we work from home, communicating only by email is not ideal. Decide for yourself how you will be able to communicate on a permanent basis. Choose an instant messaging service like Google Hangouts or Skype. If you have to work together on the same file, use document-sharing tools or a collective diary. This will save you many useless journeys and will enable you to stay in contact, sharing your ideas and point of view, or help a colleague if the occasion arises.

> "When I work at home, I stay in permanent contact with my chief editor by email. This enables us to not write about the same topics and to exchange ideas and initiatives."
> (Stephanie, journalist)

Along the same lines, do not overlook contact with the hierarchy and be present and up to date with the organisation's latest developments, even if it is only by phone. Working from home is also risking missing out on opportunities or letting new projects pass you by as you were not in the know.

To avoid this phenomenon, it is better to work one or two days per week at your place of work or, at least, to return to the office from time to time. Returning to your place of work reconciles you with your professional identity: not only do you maintain the social link with your colleagues, co-workers and superior, but you are also less likely to miss out on opportunities at work due to your physical absence.

Working too much

As we mentioned earlier, one of the greatest dangers faced by telecommuters is that of doing too much or not being able to stop. As we save time on commuting, we allow ourselves to go over our working hours, sometimes stretching our working days significantly. Having all your equipment for work available at home can harm your private life. There is a great temptation to have a quick glance at your emails, reply to some, to 'quickly' do a small task.

But being unable to disconnect and regularly going over the eight working hours can, in the long term, lead to burnout or in any case, permanent stress. This is where one of the main attractions of telecommuting, reduced stress in your professional life, disappears. This is why we keep repeating it; telecommuting is not suitable for every situation nor for all personalities. The ability to organise and motivate yourself is essential and it is also necessary to be able to create your own limits if you want to avoid burnout.

EMPLOYEE ADVICE

Do not feel guilty for working from home! Guilt can force you to do too much, to really struggle to switch off and lead to extra working hours. Refuse this pattern: just because you are working from home does not mean you do not work or you work less.

TOP TIPS

- Set yourself limits. Telecommuting does not mean extra hours and extended days. While telecommuters are quickly driven to do too much during a day of working at home, it is extremely important for your wellbeing to set necessary limits and to not let your job overflow its official time.
- Be a champion at prioritising. From the moment you start your day, it is sometimes difficult to know where to start: quickly analyse the tasks to be done during the day and prioritise them. The more important tasks will thus be finished first, you will make more progress and will remain motivated and focused.
- Celebrate when you finish a task. As homeworking involves working independently, it is important to congratulate yourself to maintain your motivation. If you need an external perspective, send an email to your colleague or your superior to receive the congratulations you need.
- Set objectives that are achievable in just one day so that you are always motivated. At the end of the day, when you look at the list of tasks you have done, you will realise the work you have got through and will be proud of what you have accomplished.
- Do not hesitate to work outside your home (at a café, a co-working space, a library, etc.). Can you no longer face being indoors? Is there a ray of sunlight outside? Take your computer and go and work outside for a few hours. Nevertheless, ensure that if you set yourself up on a terrace, for example, to only do tasks that require minimal

concentration.

- Create a pleasant working space for yourself that is comfortable and ergonomic. This will enable you to feel as if you are at the office and to be more productive.
- Disconnect. It is essential to have breaks so as to relax your brain and maintain your motivation and concentration. When we work at home, we often forget to take breaks. Yet, remember your long study periods to prepare for an exam: did you not take breaks? When telecommuting, it is the same thing; breaks are necessary to maintain a clear mind.

> "For my breaks, I make them shorter as I need them less than when I am at the office. And these breaks enable me above all to do little household chores like putting a load of laundry on or making some soup." (Stephanie, journalist)

- Regularly assess your days of telecommuting. Assess yourself after a day or week so as to see what work you have done. This will help you to see what you can improve and determine why one day was less productive than another.
- To get your daily life out of your head, write down a list of all the household tasks you have to do. If they are written down, you will think about them less. Furthermore, if you make the most of a break to do one of these tasks, it will enable you to cross it off the list and go back to work feeling more satisfied.

FAQS

WHAT ARE THE JOBS WHICH MAY REQUIRE TELECOMMUTING?

Not all jobs can be done from outside the company office. Nonetheless, thanks to the rapid development of new computer communication technologies, more and more employees are involved. Some examples are professions connected to finance, architects, computing jobs (analysts, programmers, developers, webmasters, etc.), information specialists (journalists, writers, editors, photographers), creative jobs such as publishers, graphic designers, authors, comedians, musicians, etc. In general, almost all office jobs (text handling, telemarketing, accounting, etc.) are likely to be carried out at home, but those who are most suitable are of course those whose results can be measured concretely, with the help of more or less objective indicators.

DO I HAVE TO ESTABLISH A SPECIFIC CONTRACT?

If telecommuting is not mentioned in the employee's basic contract, it is necessary to add a supplementary clause to the employment contract to explain certain agreements regarding working from home. This clause should discuss the frequency of telecommuting, times when the employee will have to be reachable and the potential reimbursement of costs for the teleworker (internet, telephone, etc.). Alongside this additional clause, the employer must explain in writing (such as by email) the tasks to be done from home and the possible report that the employee will have to provide to their superior.

IS TELECOMMUTING MORE RELAXING THAN WORKING AT THE OFFICE?

This type of work can have beneficial effects on the stress and tiredness that are caused by working life. In fact, we save (sometimes considerable) time on commuting which can be used for beneficial activities such as sleeping for an extra hour, doing sports in the morning, meditating, etc. We are also thus more relaxed and less rushed by time, traffic jams or the stress of missing our train. Furthermore, the calm atmosphere of an empty house theoretically promotes concentration, and therefore productivity, unlike the many office distractions. If we consider these factors, telecommuting can effectively turn out to be more relaxing than traditional working.

Yet, according to a study by the Rensselaer Polytechnic Institute in New York (Golden, 2011), telecommuters tend to work more from home than their colleagues at the office, sometimes at the risk of burn out. Indeed, the fact of having to be flexible and available puts telecommuters under pressure. Moreover, some people have difficulty juggling between their private and professional lives, which makes their teleworking day exhausting, as much mentally as physically.

WHAT SHOULD I DO IN THE CASE OF A COMPUTER OR HARDWARE MALFUNCTION?

The first thing to do is to let your employer and colleagues know about the malfunction that has occurred, whether it be computer software, the internet or something else. Next, the worker must do anything possible to fix the problem as quickly as possible and to inform their superior about how the repairs are advancing. The employer will nevertheless have to pay the worker even if they cannot do the work requested due to this failure.

With this in mind, it is good to be comfortable with all the tools you work with, so as to be able to quickly fix possible bugs without having to call a technician time and time again. Do not hesitate to ask your employer for training on whichever useful program you use.

WHAT HAPPENS IF THERE IS A WORK ACCIDENT?

Any accident that takes place at the place stated in the job contract or on the commute between the employee's home and their place of work is considered a work accident. This accident must also happen during the time stated on the aforementioned contract to be considered as being of a professional nature.

Meanwhile, legislation regarding work accidents in homeworking situations remains somewhat hazy and it will be up to the worker to prove that the accident happened during the execution of professional tasks. The procedure will of course be made easier if the employee is the victim of an accident in the place and during the hours that are determined in their employment contract. But in case of litigation between employer and employee on the professional or non-professional nature of the accident, the final decision will be based on the judge's discretion.

WHAT DO I DO WHEN I AM ILL?

When we regularly work from home, it is tempting to work even if we are ill, thinking that at home it will be less tiresome. Nevertheless, it is necessary to not think about the fact that we telecommute, so as to be able to really recover. There is therefore this question to be asked: "If I had to go to the office, would I be in a fit state to go there?". If the answer is no, you must consult a doctor and announce that you will be off, rather than working less well at home. In this case, it will be necessary to proceed as if you were not a teleworker: warn your employer and bring them a doctor's note as quickly as possible (if necessary).

WHAT ARE THE ASPECTS TO CONSIDER BEFORE STARTING TO TELECOMMUTE (LEGAL, PRACTICAL, LOGISTICAL AND PERSONAL ASPECTS, ETC.)?

Before launching yourself into telecommuting, it is necessary to check certain aspects in order to be sure that you are really ready.

- Firstly, the practical and logistical aspect: do you have a workspace available that is far from external and familial disturbances? Do you have a desk for working?
- From a technical perspective, can a professional computer be properly connected at your house? Does everything work or do you need to make some additional installations?
- The personal aspect must not be neglected either. Are you alone during the day? Has your family been warned that you are not available for them during office hours?
- Finally, the legal aspect is also important. It is up to you to check that a clause regarding telecommuting exists in your contract. If necessary, ask your employee to add an additional clause to your contract.

OVER TO YOU

THE FLY LADY METHOD APPLIED TO TELECOMMUTING

The idea of Fly Lady is all the rage in the United States and is, originally, aimed at housewives. The idea is to take baby steps and to organise and clean zone by zone. Applicable over one week, the Fly Lady method consists of cleaning the different rooms of the house, 15 minutes here, 15 minutes there, by following a housework plan and a list of daily tasks. Other recommendations are notably based on the establishment of a morning and evening routine and a more serious hour of tidying up once a week.

The method is applicable to teleworking, so as to develop in a tidy environment and to aid concentration. For example, make the most of a break to tidy up your desk. Tomorrow, you will attack the first drawer. The aim of the Fly Lady method is to start light and instil routines. The first week you only do one task per day. The second week, you add an additional task per day. And so forth until you overcome the disorder and integrate a daily routine to maintain order (in your folders, your emails, your desk, the monitoring of your projects, etc.).

Example of a weekly plan

Week	0	1	2	3
Monday	Prepare my planning for the week	Prepare my planning for the week; prepare a meal plan for the week and make my shopping list.	Prepare my planning and meal plan for the week; focus on my diary: what birthdays/ outings/ meetings are approaching? Are there any presents to buy or documents to print? Which weekends am I busy?	...
Tuesday	Throw out everything that is broken or unusable on my desk and tidy away things that I do not use every day.	Tidy or throw away everything that is lying around my office; do laundry.	Tidy or throw away everything that is lying around my office; do laundry; sort out my address book.	...

We want to hear from you!
Leave a comment on your online library
and share your favourite books on social media!

FURTHER READING

BIBLIOGRAPHY

- Ascento. (2015) *Télétravail et (auto-)leadership: un vrai ping-pong.* [Online]. [Accessed 15 January 2016]. Available from: <http://www.ascento.be/fr/nouvelles/detail/t%C3%A9l%C3%A9travail-et-auto-leadership-un-vrai-ping-pong>
- Ballonad Rolland, D. (2014) Bien s'organiser pour mieux travailler de chez soi. *Easy Social Media.* [Online]. [Accessed 12 December 2015]. Available from: <http://www.easy-socialmedia.com/bien-sorganiser-pour-mieux-travailler-de-chez-soi/>
- Courte, J-C. and Lukino, J. (2006) *Comment travailler... chez soi.* Paris : Eyrolles.
- Darche, C. (2015) Pourquoi les Français aiment le télétravail ? *LeFigaro.* [Online]. [Accessed 15 January 2016]. Available from: <http://www.lefigaro.fr/emploi/2015/05/10/09005-20150510ARTFIG00055-pourquoi-les-francais-aiment-le-teletravail.php>
- Golden, T. D. (2011) *Altering the Effects of Work and Family Conflict on Exhaustion: Telework During Traditional and Nontraditional Work Hours.* New York: Spring Science+Business Media LLC.
- Gombert, G. (2013) 12 conseils pour bien télétravailler. *Mode(s) d'emploi.* [Online]. [Accessed 12 December 2015]. Available from: <http://www.blog-emploi.com/12-conseils-pour-teletravailler/>
- Jobat.be. (2012) *Télétravail: ce qui est autorisé, ce qui ne l'est pas.* [Online]. [Accessed 12 December 2015].

Available from: <http://www.jobat.be/fr/articles/teletravail-ce-qui-est-autorise-ce-qui-ne-lest-pas/>

- JournalduNet.com. (2016) *Télétravail: definition et cadre juridique.* [Online]. [Accessed 4 January 2016]. Available from: <http://www.journaldunet.com/management/pratique/contrats/13934/teletravail-definition-et-cadre-juridique.html>
- Le Breton, M. (2014) Télétravail: 10 conseils pour réussir à travailler chez soi. *Le HuffPost.* [Online]. [Accessed 12 December 2015]. Available from: <http://www.huffingtonpost.fr/2014/05/09/teletravail-10-conseils-pour-reussir-a-travailler-chez-soi/>
- LeVif. (2015) *Le télétravail serait-il mauvais pour la santé?* [Online]. [Accessed 12 December 2015]. Available from: <http://www.levif.be/actualite/sante/le-teletravail-serait-il-mauvais-pour-la-sante/article-normal-440043.html>
- Robillart, O. (2014) Travail à domicile: les employés se dissent plus productifs. *Clubic pro.* [Online]. [Accessed 15 January 2016]. Available from: <http://www.clubic.com/pro/actualite-e-business/actualite-743317-employes-productifs-travaillent-maison.html>
- Tachot, A. (2010) Huit astuces pour bien débuter en télétravail. *Jeteletravaille.fr.* [Online]. [Accessed 12 December 2015]. Available from: <http://www.jeteletravaille.fr/index.php?id=1006>
- Turbé-Suetens, N. and de Mazenod, X. (2006) Petit manuel du télétravailleur. Comment s'y mettre ? *Adverbe.* [Online]. [Accessed 12 December 2015]. Available from: <http://www.adverbe.com/images/Manuel-teletravail-juillet-2006.pdf>

ADDITIONAL SOURCES

- Quinn, E. (2011) *There's No Place Like Working From Home: Get Organized, Stay Motivated, Get Things Done!* Chicago: Calloran Publishing.